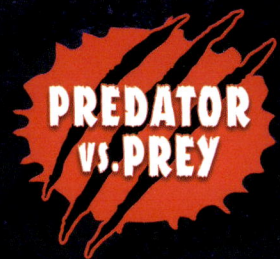

LIONS VS. ZEBRAS

FOOD CHAIN FIGHTS

BEN HUBBARD

Lerner Publications ◆ Minneapolis

For Letizia

Copyright © 2025 by Lerner Publishing Group, Inc.

All rights reserved. International copyright secured. No part of this book may be reproduced, stored in a retrieval system, or transmitted in any form or by any means—electronic, mechanical, photocopying, recording, or otherwise—without the prior written permission of Lerner Publishing Group, Inc., except for the inclusion of brief quotations in an acknowledged review.

Lerner Publications Company
An imprint of Lerner Publishing Group, Inc.
241 First Avenue North
Minneapolis, MN 55401 USA

For reading levels and more information, look up this title at www.lernerbooks.com.

Main body text set in Aptifer Sans LT Pro.
Typeface provided by Linotype AG.

Designer: Kim Morales
Lerner team: Martha Kranes

Library of Congress Cataloging-in-Publication Data

Names: Hubbard, Ben, 1973– author.
Title: Lions vs. zebras : food chain fights / Ben Hubbard.
Other titles: Lions versus zebras
Description: Minneapolis : Lerner Publications, [2025] | Series: Predator vs. prey | Includes bibliographical references and index. | Audience: Ages 8–11 | Audience: Grades 4–6 | Summary: "Head into the savannas and grasslands where lions and zebras roam. Discover a battle between predator and prey. Young readers learn more about each animal's strengths and weaknesses and find out who wins the fight"— Provided by publisher.
Identifiers: LCCN 2023039251 (print) | LCCN 2023039252 (ebook) | ISBN 9798765626764 (library binding) | ISBN 9798765629390 (paperback) | ISBN 9798765636244 (epub)
Subjects: LCSH: Lion—Juvenile literature. | Zebras—Juvenile literature. | Predation (Biology)—Juvenile literature. | Camouflage (Biology)—Juvenile literature. | Food chains (Ecology)—Juvenile literature.
Classification: LCC QL737.C23 H83 2025 (print) | LCC QL737.C23 (ebook) | DDC 599.665/7—dc23/eng/20231204

LC record available at https://lccn.loc.gov/2023039251
LC ebook record available at https://lccn.loc.gov/2023039252

Manufactured in the United States of America
2-1012935-52007-6/18/2025

TABLE OF CONTENTS

CHAPTER 1
HIGH PLAINS CHASE — 4

CHAPTER 2
LIONS VS. ZEBRAS — 8

CHAPTER 3
RULER OF THE PLAINS — 24

PREDATOR VS. PREY: HEAD-TO-HEAD — 28

GLOSSARY — 30

LEARN MORE — 31

INDEX — 32

CHAPTER 1
HIGH PLAINS CHASE

THE SKY DARKENS AS THE SUN SETS ON THE AFRICAN PLAINS. A herd of zebras grazes on the grass. The zebras move slowly and keep their heads low. Their ears turn in different directions to listen for trouble. This helps them stay safe, but danger is near.

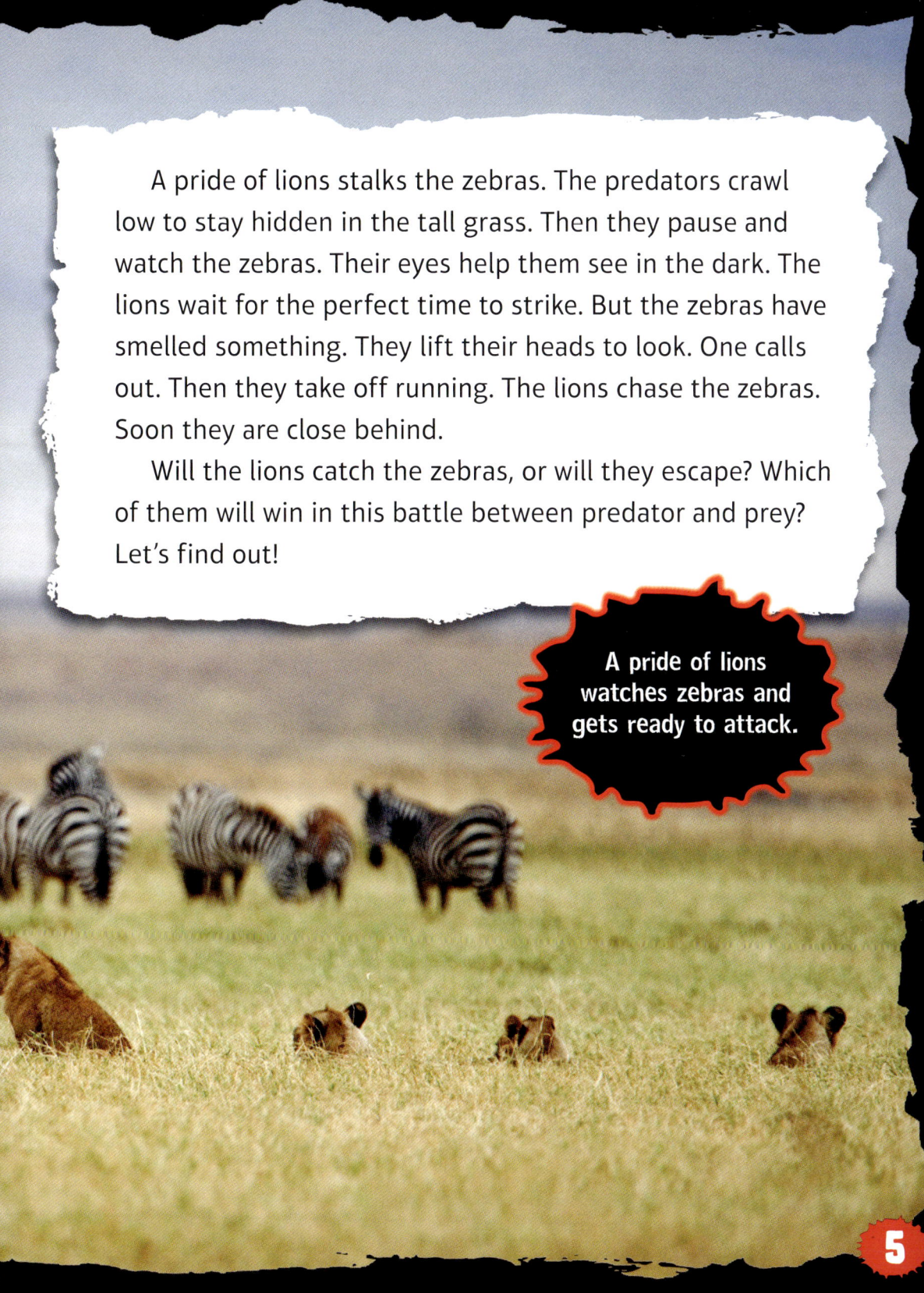

A pride of lions stalks the zebras. The predators crawl low to stay hidden in the tall grass. Then they pause and watch the zebras. Their eyes help them see in the dark. The lions wait for the perfect time to strike. But the zebras have smelled something. They lift their heads to look. One calls out. Then they take off running. The lions chase the zebras. Soon they are close behind.

Will the lions catch the zebras, or will they escape? Which of them will win in this battle between predator and prey? Let's find out!

A pride of lions watches zebras and gets ready to attack.

Zebras and lions live in Africa's vast plains and grasslands. Lions are one of the greatest land predators. They are called the king of beasts. Lions are unique in the big-cat kingdom. This is because they live in prides. Most big cats live on their own.

Prides have between four and thirty-seven members. They spend the day resting and part of the night hunting. Lions hunt animals such as wildebeests, antelopes, and zebras. They are excellent hunters, but their prey also have tough defenses that make them hard to catch.

A zebra's best defense is its herd. Each herd is made up of several families. A family has one male, several females, and their young. Zebras are herbivores. Some herds have up to a thousand members. Zebras spend most of their time walking and eating grass. But they can still stand up against lions.

The zebras and lions are both ready for battle. But which animal has what it takes to win?

DAZZLING ZEBRAS
A group of zebras can be called a herd, zeal, or dazzle.

LION STATS

WEIGHT: 265 to 570 pounds (120 to 260 kg)

LENGTH: 5.3 to 8 feet (1.6 to 2.4 m)

TOP SPEED: up to 50 miles (80 km) an hour

ZEBRA STATS

WEIGHT: 350 to 992 pounds (159 to 450 kg)

LENGTH: 7.2 to 8.2 feet (2.2 to 2.5 m)

TOP SPEED: 40 miles (64 km) an hour

CHAPTER 2
LIONS VS. ZEBRAS

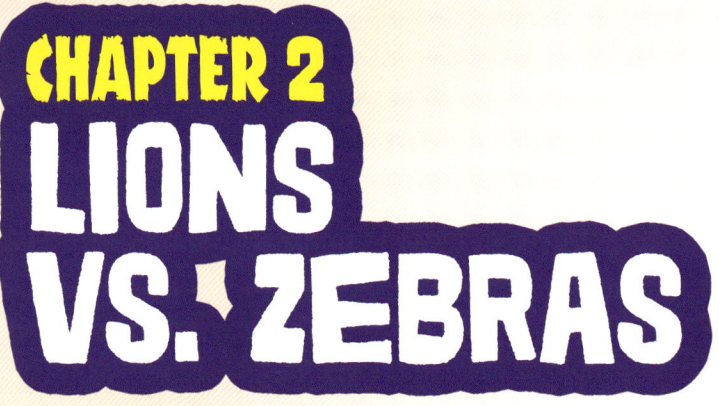

LIONS AND ZEBRAS HAVE MANY STRENGTHS TO HELP THEM STAY ALIVE. But which rules the African plains? Let's compare the animals to see!

STRENGTH

Lions are powerful predators. They have long, muscular bodies and big paws. Their short, strong legs are perfect for leaping. At the end of their legs are paws with sharp claws. Each claw can reach 1.5 inches (3.8 cm) long. Lions use their claws to grab onto prey.

LOUD LIONS
A lion's roar can be heard from 5 miles (8 km) away

A lioness stands strong beside cubs.

A zebra kicks to defend itself.

Zebras are strong animals with powerful legs and hooves as hard as hammers. Zebras have a deadly kick. They also have superstrong skin on their behinds. This skin is covered with thick hair. The hair and skin are hard for a lion to bite through.

COLOR

Zebras' black coats are lined with white. The stripes help keep the animal cool by reflecting the sun. They also confuse horseflies, which bite the zebras. Some experts say the stripes may make it harder for lions to see them in a herd.

Lions have yellow, brown, and orange coats. The coloring helps them blend in with tall, brown grass. This makes them hard to see. Male lions have hair around their heads called a mane. Their manes might help to attract females. Females do most of the hunting.

A lioness camouflages with the brown grass.

MIND MY SMELL

Lions pee on bushes and trees to mark their territory.

SENSES

Lions have strong senses. They have a special organ on the roofs of their mouths that helps them smell. They open their mouths to better smell prey. Lion eyes reflect light to help them see at night. They often hunt at dusk, at dawn, or at night. Their ears move from side to side when listening for sounds. They can hear sounds from more than 1 mile (1.6 km) away.

Lions open their mouths and wrinkle their noses to help them smell.

Zebras' eyes help them see movement from far away.

Zebras use their senses to look out for danger. Their ears move in every direction to pick up sounds from miles away. These sounds include birds, which cry out when predators are close. Zebras also have amazing senses of smell and sight. Eyes on the sides of their heads give them a wide range of vision. Their eyes also work well in low light, which helps them see at night. Zebras often smell a predator before they see it.

A lioness leaps as she chases prey.

SPEED

Lions can sprint at 50 miles (80 km) an hour. That's nearly twice as fast as the fastest human! But lions can't run fast for long. If a lion doesn't catch its prey quickly, it soon runs out of energy.

Zebras are speedy animals and can run as fast as 40 miles (64 km) an hour. This is slower than a lion. But zebras can maintain the speed over a longer distance. They can often outrun an attacking lion.

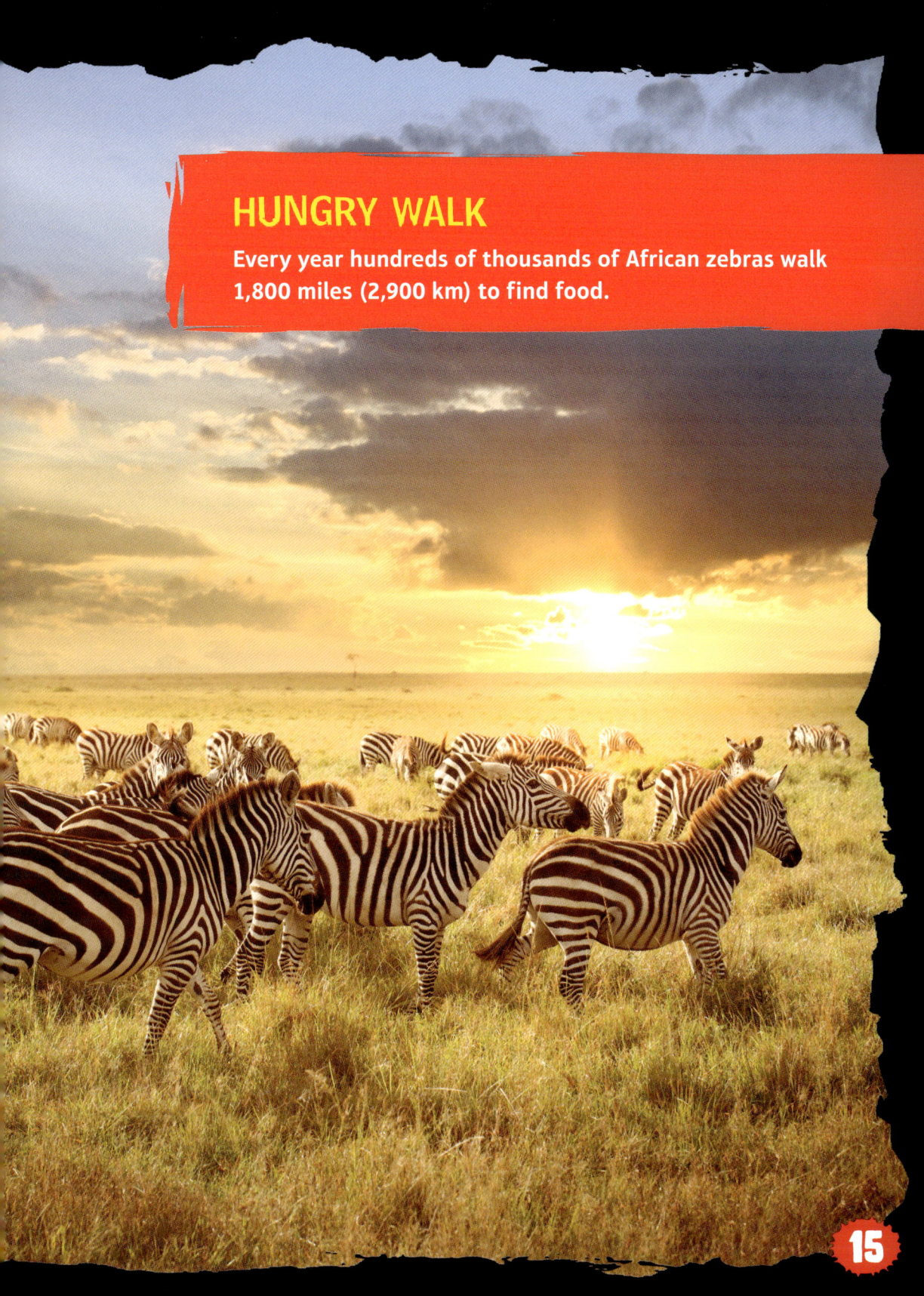

HUNGRY WALK

Every year hundreds of thousands of African zebras walk 1,800 miles (2,900 km) to find food.

LAZY LIONS

Lions spend about twenty-one hours a day resting.

KEY WEAPONS

Lions have powerful jaws and about thirty sharp teeth. They use their teeth to tear through skin and flesh. Lions have teeth up to 2.8 inches (7 cm) long. They bite off chunks of meat and swallow them whole.

A lion shows off his teeth as he roars.

Most adult zebras have forty teeth.

A zebra's best weapons are its teeth and kick. Zebras have sharp teeth to cut and eat grass. But they also use them to bite predators. Zebras also have muscular legs and hard hooves. They can knock out a lion or kill it with a well-aimed kick.

Lionesses attack a buffalo.

FINDING FOOD

Lions work together to find their food. They hide in long grass to stalk their prey. Lions are experts at keeping low and crawling quickly. They pick out a single animal and surround it. They move in close. They sprint toward the prey and strike. Then they can eat.

Zebras spend up to twenty-two hours a day eating. Zebras mainly feed on grass, but they also eat twigs, leaves, and even bark. While the herd eats, male zebras stay near the back to look out for predators. They call out when danger is near. Then the herd gets ready to fight or flee.

Zebras graze on grass.

ZEBRA TEETH
Zebras' big, flat teeth are perfect for picking and eating grass.

ATTACKS AND DEFENSES

Lions attack by sprinting at their prey and jumping on them. They can leap 36 feet (11 m) through the air to grab tall prey. The lion bites its prey's throat and neck to bring it down. Other lions join in. Once the prey is dead, the pride eats it on the spot.

A lion leaps atop a buffalo.

MASSIVE MEALS
A lion can eat more than 75 pounds (34 kg) in a single meal.

Zebras circle around a lioness.

Zebras defend one another. When an attacker is near, they form a semicircle to face it. The zebras keep their heads low, ears back, and teeth bared. The zebras kick and bite the predator. The herd will form a circle around an injured zebra to protect it.

WEAKNESSES

Lions are known for their speed. But they can only sprint for about 328 feet (100 m). They have to be close to their prey to catch it. If they attack too far away, their hunt will fail. They often don't catch their prey. Then they have to rest before trying again.

A lioness resting in a tree

DIGGING TO DRINK
Zebras often dig in dried-up riverbeds to find underground water.

A zebra's weakness is having to eat often. So zebras are always looking for food in places where predators may be nearby. A zebra is usually protected by its herd. But if it strays outside of the herd, it is in danger. Predators such as lions can easily spot young, sick, or old zebras. These zebras have little chance on their own against a lion pride.

When a zebra is on its own, it has to watch for predators.

CHAPTER 3
RULER OF THE PLAINS

AS THE ZEBRAS RUN FROM THE LIONS, ONE FALLS BEHIND. The young zebra tries to keep up with the herd but falls farther and farther behind. Several lions surround the zebra. One leaps on top and tries to bite its neck. But the lion falls off. Some zebras turn to see if they can help.

But it is too late. Another lion rushes forward. It grabs the zebra's throat and bites hard. The zebra falls to its knees. The fight is over. The lion pride gathers around the kill and take turns eating. The zebra herd races away from the danger.

A lioness chases a young zebra.

Lions and zebras are both tough animals that are up for a fight. They watch out for others in their group on the African plains. Lions are one of the top predators on land. They are armed to take down large prey. Few other hunters have their size, strength, and speed.

Yet zebras are well equipped to fend off lions. They are fast, fierce, and protected by their herds. Zebras can also land a fatal kick if cornered. Lions must be cautious when attacking zebras. They pick off a single member. Even then, a kill is not guaranteed.

Zebras sometimes sprint away from a lion attack.

Lions have to hunt and eat other animals to live.

The lions won this battle of the African habitat. They will not need to hunt again for a week. But next time, who knows? The zebras may fight the lions off, and they will have to go hungry. The story of survival continues.

PREDATOR VS. PREY: HEAD-TO-HEAD

LION
- Powerful jaws and sharp teeth for attack
- Long claws to grab and grip prey

ZEBRA
- Strong legs and hard hooves for killer kicks
- Spade-shaped teeth for brutal bites

GLOSSARY

dusk: the period between the end of the day and night

fatal: deadly

flesh: the soft parts of an animal's body

graze: to eat grass, sometimes growing in a field

habitat: the place or home where an animal or plant naturally lives and grows

herbivore: an animal that only eats plants, not meat

predator: an animal that hunts and kills other animals for food

prey: an animal that is hunted and killed for food

sense: how an animal understands its surroundings. Senses include touch, smell, taste, sight, and hearing.

LEARN MORE

Britannica Kids: Zebra
https://kids.britannica.com/kids/article/zebra/353951

Gillespie, Katie. *Zebra*. New York: Lightbox Learning, 2023.

Gish, Melissa. *Zebras*. Mankato, MN: Creative Education, 2024.

Markle, Sandra. *On the Hunt with Lions*. Minneapolis: Lerner Publications, 2023.

National Geographic Kids: Lion
https://kids.nationalgeographic.com/animals/mammals/facts/lion

National Geographic Kids: Zebra
https://kids.nationalgeographic.com/animals/mammals/facts/zebra

INDEX

attack, 14, 20, 22, 26

bites, 10, 16–17, 20–21, 24–25

danger, 4, 13, 19, 23, 25

ears, 4, 12–13, 21

grass, 4–6, 11, 17–19

herd, 4, 6, 10, 19, 21, 23–26

hooves, 10, 17

kick, 10, 17, 21, 26

plains, 4, 6, 8, 26

predators, 5–6, 8, 13, 17, 19, 21, 23, 26

prey, 5–6, 8, 12, 14, 18, 20, 22, 26

pride, 5–6, 20, 23, 25

sprint, 14, 18, 20, 22

strength, 8, 26

teeth, 16–17, 19, 21

vision, 13

PHOTO ACKNOWLEDGMENTS

Image credits: Panoramic Images/Alamy, pp. 4–5; Maggy Meyer/Shutterstock, p. 7 (top); Debbie Aird Designs/Shutterstock, p. 7 (bottom); Vicki Jauron, Babylon and Beyond Photography/Getty Images, pp. 8–9, 23; Paul Souders/Getty Images, p. 10; Peter Betts/Shutterstock, p. 11; SteffenTravel/Shutterstock, p. 12; Henrik Sorensen/Getty Images, p. 13; Martin Harvey/Getty Images, p. 14; narvikk/Getty Images, p. 15; COULANGES/Shutterstock, p. 16; Joe McDonald/Getty Images, p. 17; AfriPics.com/Alamy, p. 18; Andrzej Kubik/Shutterstock, p. 19; AOosthuizen/Getty Images, p. 20; Kakuli/Shutterstock, p. 21; PRILL/Shutterstock, p. 22; Graham Needham/Shutterstock, p. 24–25; GP232/Getty Images, p. 26; Ozkan Ozmen/Getty Images, p. 27; Ana Gram/Shutterstock, p. 28; MogensTrolle/Getty Images, p. 29. Design elements: iunewind/Shutterstock; Milano M/Shutterstock; Ukrainian studio/Shutterstock; Cassel/Shutterstock; Textures and backgrounds/Shutterstock; Print Net/Shutterstock.

Cover: Anup Shah/Getty Images; James Warwick/Getty Images.